Original title:
Life, Love, and Confusion

Copyright © 2025 Creative Arts Management OÜ
All rights reserved.

Author: Clara Whitfield
ISBN HARDBACK: 978-1-80566-170-2
ISBN PAPERBACK: 978-1-80566-465-9

The Colors of Enigma

In a world of mismatched socks,
We dance on floors with squeaky clocks,
Pies taste funny when they're not sweet,
And laughter's found on sticky feet.

Chasing shadows that tease the mind,
A riddle wrapped with answers blind,
Colors swirl like a painter's spree,
Yet all we grasp is mystery.

A Love Not Yet Defined

A wink in the dark, a glimmering grin,
We toss around hearts like confetti in wind,
Plans for dinner that never went right,
Yet here we are, in quirky delight.

We text in riddles and play hide and seek,
Can we make sense of this silly technique?
Our conversations are jigsawed face,
Connecting pieces in a peculiar race.

Exploring the Abyss of the Heart

As we tiptoe on marshmallow clouds,
The echoes of giggles form playful crowds,
We dive into puzzles with mismatched keys,
Unraveling knots in the briskest breeze.

With each twist of fate, the map goes awry,
Balloons float higher, the ground waves goodbye,
Yet, amidst the chaos, there's joy to be found,
A treasure map drawn on the upside-down ground.

The Flickering Flame of Ambivalence

A candle flickers like a tongue-in-cheek,
As we stumble through moments, both bold and meek,
In choices so tangled, we can't find our way,
Yet we giggle and chuckle, come what may.

Love letters written in invisible ink,
Do we soar high or swim in the brink?
With confetti storms and candy canes,
We dance in circles, embracing the rains.

Intersections of Fate

Two paths cross, a clumsy shuffle,
One spilled drink, laughter bursts in a bubble.
A glance exchanged, an awkward stare,
Trip on thoughts, we tumble, unaware.

Forecasts predict a sunny delight,
But clouds of doubt creep in at night.
We dance in circles, bump and glide,
Navigating chaos with arms open wide.

Murmurs of an Untold Story

Whispers linger, secrets collide,
In crowded rooms where we try to hide.
A wink, a nod, a coded tease,
Chasing shadows with charming ease.

Laughter echoes, a digital flare,
Texting riddles from anywhere.
We're all lost in this fun charade,
Romantic comedies we haven't made.

The Map of Yearning

Point A to B, a map gone wild,
GPS says turn, I'm just a child.
Lost in traffic, we giggle and pout,
As dreams of destinations flit about.

An arrow spins, the compass is shy,
Underneath stars, with a wink and a sigh.
We chart our course with adventurous whim,
Finding treasures in the chances we swim.

Threads of an Uncertain Tapestry

Stitch by stitch, we weave the wrong way,
Colorful chaos on a fraying display.
Laughter woven in every seam,
Life's little mishaps, a quirky dream.

Knots and tangles, patterns collide,
Our misfit tapestry, with cheeks that are wide.
In the fabric of glee, we fret and we fumble,
Celebrating the art of our splendid stumble.

Echoes in a Wistful Dream

In the realm of wobbly chairs,
Words slip like jellybeans.
I chase after tangled thoughts,
While my coffee dances, it seems.

A sock speaks in riddles loud,
But who am I to judge?
Tiptoeing through the crooked maze,
With a well-meaning grudge.

Balloons float with cheeky grins,
As puppies plot behind,
Whispers of cake and dance parties,
Leave stitched smiles on my mind.

So here we twirl, in a spin,
Gathering joy wrapped in haste,
Like candy tossed to the sky,
Confetti of dreams interlaced.

Portraits of an Unraveled Soul

The mirror giggles at my face,
With toothpaste on one cheek.
I search for meaning between the cracks,
But it seems the answers are weak.

Puddle reflections break and sway,
As I hop like a curious frog.
What genius decided it's fun
To unravel like a worn-out blog?

In the closet, secrets yearn,
As dust bunnies have a ball.
I wear my mismatched shoes with pride,
Still unsure at the shopping mall.

With each twist and every turn,
My thoughts dance like wavy lines.
They swirl in a brilliant chaos,
As laughter rings, love maligns.

The Labyrinth of Us

Two squirrels arguing over nuts,
While I find my left shoe.
Maps drawn with a crayon,
Guide me to where dreams brew.

Chasing shadows of ice cream cones,
That vanish in sunny rays.
Where did we put our thoughts again?
They rolled away in a haze.

Questions bounce on trampoline hearts,
Springing into the air.
Do turtles sing when they see stars?
Life spins without a care.

Through the maze, we laugh and spin,
A dance of dizzy delight.
Each corner holds a new surprise,
As we twinkle into the night.

Kaleidoscope of Dilemmas

Jigsaw pieces of purple jelly,
Never fit in the box.
Who brought these spicy pickles?
The surprise is what shocks.

Tangled hair in the morning light,
A hat with feathers takes flight.
Why did I choose socks like this?
Oh, well, it adds to the sight.

Colors clash like silly jokes,
Dancing through the air like dreams.
A saxophone squeaks out a laugh,
As chaos bursts at the seams.

In this swirling, twirling world,
Each moment is a cheerful blend.
Our hearts chuckle in the maze,
With whimsy that never ends.

Unwritten Chapters

In a book without a cover, I write,
Sticky notes and crumpled dreams in sight.
Coffee spills and laughter in each line,
Characters twist while sipping cheap wine.

Plot twists dance like socks on the floor,
Unexpected visits, keys locked, just more.
The cat, a critic, purring with disdain,
On plots that wander like a runaway train.

A hero stumbles into the wrong scene,
While villains plot while sipping green cuisine.
With every page turned, the hiccups thrive,
A comedy show where pages come alive.

Yet through the chaos comes a silver thread,
Woven through anecdotes of what is said.
In every scribble, a heartbeat's embrace,
Unfinished sentences, a wild chase.

The Flicker of Connection

A wink sent over coffee, oh so bold,
Muffin crumbs of secrets yet untold.
Eyes meet in the chaos, hearts take flight,
Awkward small talk, a comical delight.

The groove of timing, a dance misled,
Tripping over words, blushes turn red.
A nudge, a laugh; does it mean the same?
Like playing charades in a secret game.

Tangled in thoughts, the nerves do race,
Tacos for dinner, such questionable taste.
Yet amid the giggles, sparks start to glow,
In the flicker of moments, connections flow.

If only the universe would send a sign,
Like a huge flashing neon, "She's partly mine!"
Yet we laugh and tease, meeting halfway,
In this whimsical whirl, we drift and play.

Between the Waves of Feeling

Oh, the tides of what we think we know,
Riding the waves in a charming row.
Highs and lows like socks lost at sea,
What's clear as day is a riddle to me.

You smile, but what's behind that grin?
An ocean of thoughts, where to begin?
Drifting like boats on a windy day,
Amongst whispers of what words can't say.

Splashes of joy and dustings of doubt,
Catch you off guard when you're flipping out.
Like dancing in puddles, what's wrong and right,
Twists and turns that leave us in flight.

Yet through the muddle, each droplet will show,
In the laughter and chaos, the truth in the flow.
With every wave crashing, a new chance to glide,
Between what we feel and the silly ride.

Crescendo of Doubt

A chorus of questions starts to bloom,
Playful whispers beneath the same moon.
Is it a spark or a glitch in the plot?
Every answer found leads to yet another knot.

Confetti of thoughts flies in the air,
As blunders lead to moments so rare.
A crescendo builds, but where does it land?
In the symphony of awkward, we take a stand.

The notes get sharper when we try to connect,
Like two left feet in a dance we suspect.
Yet there's magic in how we trip on our way,
Laughter erupts, come what may.

As we spiral through humor and jumbled phrases,
The melody catches us in heartfelt phases.
So let's embrace the clamor, the doubt, and the cheer,
In this funny crescendo, we hold what is dear.

The Weight of Unsaid Goodbyes

In the silence, we nod and smile,
With thoughts trapped in a tangled aisle.
A wave from afar, a wink in lieu,
Did we just say hello or adieu?

The cake was great, but where's the fork?
We're lost in chatter, but where's the cork?
Each glance is a script with lines unplayed,
To leave it all unsaid, did we misplace?

We dance around truths like squirrels with nuts,
Hiding our hearts in oversized guts.
With every missed word, we laugh and sigh,
Should we write a letter, or let it fly?

The weight of what's not said is a heavy load,
Like socks with holes on a long, damp road.
Yet here we are, with lemon zest cheer,
Sipping on memories, one blurry tear.

Sketches of Intimacy

Your laugh is a brush, painting the night,
While I juggle my thoughts, unsure if it's right.
But we're sketching our dreams with crayons and clay,
In this gallery of whispers, we might lose our way.

You say I'm a puzzle, with pieces askew,
I say you're an artist, what should we do?
Between giggles and glances, oh what a mess,
Is this how it feels to be in distress?

We scribble in margins, where doodles collide,
Each line a confession we try to hide.
It's messy and awkward, yet oh-so sincere,
In this gallery of gaffes, no need to fear.

We trace every wrinkle, every odd crease,
Creating a mural of chaos and peace.
In this funny affair, our hearts are the frame,
Together in sketches, we're never the same.

Between Dreams and Reality

In the land where the socks always lose their mate,
I wander in circles, it feels like fate.
Chasing the rainbow, it slips from my hand,
Is it just a mirage, or something so grand?

My mind makes promises, like 'get up and shine,'
But my bed has become a personal shrine.
With visions of dragons and pancakes so tall,
Reality blinks, is it a dream after all?

The clock's ticking loud, yet I lay like a toad,
Time flies like an owl, when it's on the road.
Between sleepy giggles and dreams that ignite,
I wrestle the day while embracing the night.

So here I remain, in this strange little space,
Where jesters and dreams often engage in a race.
With pistachio sunsets and jellybean skies,
Who knew that the funny could come as a surprise?

A Journey in Between

Packed bags of confusion, I'm off on a quest,
With maps full of doodles, I'm feeling quite blessed.
In this middle of nowhere, I find a lost sock,
It seems even the laundry is taking a walk.

Each step feels like dancing, though the beat's out of tune,

I'm hugging this moment beneath a bright moon.
With sandwiches stacked up, and stories to share,
Every silly mishap, a breath of fresh air.

The road's like a puzzle, both crooked and neat,
With strangers who wave, and unexpected treats.
Oh, the things that will happen, just wait and you'll see,
In this journey of nonsense, we'll finally flee.

So here's to the chaos, the giggles, the fun,
In this carnival circus, where everyone runs.
I smile at the skids and the silly detours,
For it's in these odd moments, adventure endures.

Serenade of Misty Dreams

In a world where socks go rogue,
And cats start wearing shoes,
I try to make my bed each day,
But pillows plot to snooze.

The coffee spills, a morning stunt,
I trip on freshly mopped floors,
Yet laughter fills the air quite loud,
As chaos gently soars.

In transit on a jammed train ride,
I find a seat and grin,
A stranger's smile, a twist of fate,
We're both lost in the din.

And when the stars begin to wink,
I'll dance with all my dreams,
For in this funny jumble,
Life's more than what it seems.

Dancing in the Gray

Under clouds shaped like silly hats,
We whirl and spin like tops,
With mismatched shoes and wobbly moves,
We chuckle till we drop.

A pigeon seeks my sandwich,
As I wave it off with grace,
My comfort food's now under siege,
At the park's unkind embrace.

Yet in this dance of giggles lost,
Embrace the quirky plight,
For in the muddle of it all,
There's joy in our shared fight.

So let the music play quite loud,
With rhythms out of place,
We'll twirl through life's amusing game,
With smiles upon our face.

Illusions of Togetherness

We picnic on a blanket spread,
But ants are in revolt,
One friend brought potato salad,
Another brought the jolt.

As laughter fills the balmy air,
A breeze whisks all away,
Our plans scatter like wayward kites,
Yet we still want to stay.

The drinks are fizzy, chats are loud,
We sip and spill with glee,
A dog steals half my sandwich bite,
And chases a bee.

In moments where we're lost for words,
We nod in knowing cheer,
For in the madness of our time,
Together, we find dear.

Splintered Reflections

Mirrors show a fractured view,
With hairdos stuck in time,
A shirt mismatch makes me smile,
Am I a wizard in my prime?

As echoes of my thoughts collide,
A jumble that won't stop,
I trip over my yesterday,
Then tumble on a mop.

The clock keeps ticking offbeat tunes,
While I search for matching socks,
The world spins on, a dance gone wrong,
Yet joy fills up the blocks.

So watch me as I juggle hope,
With laughter in my stride,
For splinters in reflections bright,
Are just a funny ride.

An Odyssey of Heart

In a circus of whispers, we dance on a line,
With jumbled up thoughts, like dogs in a pine.
Each glance is a puzzle, a riddle to crack,
As we trip over feelings, we always look back.

Laughter spills over like coffee on jeans,
While juggling decisions, we're lost in our dreams.
With a wink and a nod, we spin like a top,
In this wild, wobbly world, we never will stop.

The Map of Unseen Places

In the maze of affection, we wander and roam,
With GPS hearts that refuse to feel home.
Each twist and each turn leads to chuckles and sighs,
Like stars in a fart cloud, we light up the skies.

Coffee spills over maps, our markers are thin,
Finding roads in the laughter, where does it begin?
With scribbles of chaos, we sketch out the fun,
In this journey we're on, we've only just begun.

Tracing Paths in Turmoil

Like squirrels in a maze, we dart and we dash,
Our thoughts are like kids, forever a clash.
With pranks up our sleeves, and jokes on the go,
We stumble through moments, embracing the flow.

Chaos our companion, we navigate mess,
With giggles and grumbles, we secretly bless.
In the oddest of corners, we find what is real,
Sailing through tempests, all tangled up, we wheel.

The Language of Fleeting Moments

With winks and a chuckle, we toss out our bets,
Communication's a dance, full of slips and regrets.
We rhyme without reason, our punchlines offbeat,
In a world of warm chaos, we tango on feet.

Jokes float like bubbles, then pop with a laugh,
Each second a snapshot, a quirky gaffe.
In the art of confusion, where clarity hides,
We scribble our hopes on the whimsical tides.

Rays of Unfamiliar Light

In the morning, I spill my tea,
Wondering how it ended up on me.
Sunshine giggles from the sky,
As I ponder how cats learn to fly.

The toast pops up with a cheerful dance,
While my socks are lost in a strange romance.
Butterflies mock my breakfast choice,
And cucumbers grumble—no one hears their voice.

Late at night, my thoughts take flight,
Like a squirrel who thinks he's a knight.
Dance parties are held by the dust,
But they leave me lonely, I must adjust.

A pickle jar holds all my dreams,
Forgotten under whimsical themes.
The cat just yawns, unbothered, it seems,
While I'm left chasing my glittering beams.

Facades and Fragments

A jester slips on a banana peel,
While I juggle my hopes, trying to feel.
The mirror's full of winks and sighs,
Reflecting my strange desire to fly.

Wearing masks of polka dots, I prance,
In a world where no one knows how to dance.
Rain clouds float by with a knowing grin,
As I try to dance without stepping in.

I ask a fish what's under its scales,
It flops in giggles, telling tall tales.
As the clock strikes twelve, chaos sings,
And the unmade bed sprouts glittery wings.

With socks mismatched in a colorful game,
I stride through this world feeling quite the same.
A riddle or puzzle, a tickle or tease,
Life giggles at me, begging me to sneeze.

Chasing Fleeting Shadows

A shadow dances with a twirl and spin,
As I chase after it wearing a grin.
Lattes confuse me, hot or cold?
I sip and ponder tales untold.

A rabbit hops by with no care at all,
Telling secrets of a grand masquerade ball.
The sun holds a mirror, laughing outright,
While I cover my face, shy from the light.

Kites in the sky seem too smart to land,
As I sit with spaghetti that slips from my hand.
The breeze carries whispers of things gone askew,
While my hat floats further from me than I knew.

With jellybeans in pockets, I pursue the unknown,
Wishing on stars from my comfy throne.
What's real, what's faux? A parade made of dreams,
In this circus of nonsense, nothing's as it seems.

The Alchemy of Missing Pieces

A puzzle piece wanders, lost in my coat,
Vying for glory with a potato that wrote.
Goldfish giggle in bubbles of cheer,
While I wear a hat made of leftovers, oh dear!

Lost socks conspire to form a new crew,
With tea bags debating what's brewing anew.
Bookmarks throw parties by the stair,
Where old receipts gossip without a care.

A ghost once visited, claimed it had style,
Sipped on my coffee and stayed for a while.
Cereal boxes whisper secrets at night,
While I chase my thoughts, just out of sight.

Magic awaits in the crumbs on the floor,
As I laugh with the cat who just opened the door.
In the midst of chaos, a truth still escapes,
That joy is the puzzle that forever shapes.

Serendipity in Shadows

In a cafe, I lost my way,
Tripped on my thoughts, bright as day.
Coffee spilled, a new fashion,
Laughter danced in sweet distraction.

Umbrellas rain down in a swirl,
Chasing the cupcake with a twirl.
Found a penny, made a wish,
What a day for a silly twist!

A pigeon stole my sandwich away,
I guess it wanted to play.
Forgot my phone, what a bummer,
But then I met a guy named Summer.

With a wink, he spun a tale,
Of dragons, ships, and winds to sail.
In shadows where golden sun meets,
We chuckled at our tangled feats.

Chasing Fleeting Moments

The clock ticks loud, mocking the chase,
I tripped over shoes in the wrong place.
Snatched a chip from a passing snack,
Oops! Swallowed wrong — I'll be right back!

Yesterday's outfit, who knew it would fit?
Tangled in threads, a stylish split.
Every misstep, a dance so grand,
Two left feet in a one-legged stand.

Glimpses of laughter, let's capture the charm,
With a silly picture, I'll sound the alarm.
Life's just a ride through a quirky fair,
With whispers and giggles floating in the air.

Hold tight to moments, they slip through the cracks,
Like socks in the dryer, they never come back.
Yet here we are, we forge ahead,
With smiles in our pockets and crumbs from bread.

Heartstrings and Hidden Paths

They say to follow your heart's little tug,
But mine's on a journey — it's lost in a mug.
First dates with pizza, oh what a dream!
Yet I spat out my soda, a hiccuping beam.

Chasing smiles through each twist and bend,
Fumbled a greeting, forgot how to send.
We played charades with awkward delight,
Under the table, our laughter took flight.

Sticky notes filled with arrows and art,
Mapping the patterns that tug at the heart.
Every squiggle, a story to tell,
Of mishaps and giggles — oh, can't you tell?

In crowded rooms where echoes collide,
We find little corners where silliness hides.
Each moment a puzzle, each smile a piece,
In the grand tapestry, we find our release.

A Symphony of Hurts and Hopes

In the orchestra pit, my shoes tap away,
A violin screeches, oh what a display!
With twirls and twists, we fumble the tune,
Even the moon's giggling over the dune.

Puppies chasing tails round the picnic spread,
Found a half-eaten sandwich — no tears to shed.
Musicians arguing over the right note,
While I serenade dreams from a rubber boat.

Lost my keys in a wild game of chase,
Under the couch, they danced with lace.
Every misstep, a joyous refrain,
With hiccups of joy lapsing into the sane.

Watch the confetti, it sprinkles the air,
A symphony plays — it's beyond compare.
Through struggles and giggles, we sing our ballads,
Creating a chorus that never quite mallets.

Whispers of the Heart

A cat on the roof and a hat on the floor,
Chasing my thoughts like a dog at the door.
Socks in the dryer, but where did they go?
Heart's in a tumble, but putting on a show.

Pizza for breakfast, who made this decree?
Pancakes for dinner? It's fine, let it be!
Mom said, 'Be neat,' but have you seen my room?
Scribbles on paper, I'll make it my bloom.

When questions come knocking, I open the door,
Each answer spins wild, like a dance on the floor.
Do you feel the sunshine, or just the cold air?
Tell me your secrets while I fix my hair.

So let's toast to the quirks and the silly mistakes,
Juggling laughter like we're riding on bikes.
In this carnival life, we'll wear clownish grins,
For joy is a riddle, our game just begins.

Threads of Uncertainty

A sock puppet sings in a hat made of cheese,
As questions swirl round like leaves in the breeze.
Jellybean dreams and a marshmallow shout,
What is it all about? Let's figure it out!

Dancing with shadows, they step on my toes,
Each misstep just adds to the curious prose.
Why does the toaster refuse me a slice?
Maybe it's shy, or it thinks I'm too nice.

With googly eyes, I gaze at my cake,
It simples the truth: it's a bizarre little bake.
Fingers in frosting, I laugh and I twirl,
These whims of the heart get you spinning in swirls.

Let's hop on a train that goes nowhere fast,
Through tunnels of quandary, we're free at last.
In this jumbled adventure with glitter and noise,
We'll chuckle through chaos, that's how we find joy!

Dance of Endless Questions

Tickle my brain with a puzzling charade,
Why does it rain when I've got a parade?
I'll wear my galoshes with style and with flair,
Who needs an umbrella? I'll dance in despair!

Pinching the moon with my fingertips tight,
What's the reason for stars amid the night?
If time could be candy, I'd gobble it whole,
But that pesky calorie counts take their toll.

Whispers of dreams float like jelly on toast,
What happens to dreams when we stop them the most?
Wearing mismatched shoes on this fanciful street,
With each silly question, we waltz to the beat.

So gather your giggles, let's spin tales galore,
With jests made from giggles and talks about yore.
In this circus of thoughts, we'll tumble and roll,
For finding the punchline is how we feel whole!

Tangles in the Garden of Feelings

In a garden of whispers, I stumbled on words,
Butterflies giggle, and sunshine disturbs.
Petals of laughter sprinkled on grass,
Why do daisies always seem to have class?

Hopping like bunnies through tangled up vines,
Every twisty question aligns with the pines.
I tried to plant wishes; they sprouted a joke,
Quantum puzzlers in the stem of a choke.

Pounding my head with a spoon on the table,
Should I write a story or just make a fable?
Dirt on my fingers, oh, what a fine mess,
Still trying to find where I buried my stress.

So tiptoe through chaos, and picnic with fun,
Share secrets and giggles; our time has begun.
The weeds may grow wild, but so will the smiles,
In this zany garden, we'll wander for miles.

Puzzle Pieces of Affection

We fit together, like socks and shoes,
Yet sometimes it feels like I've lost my muse.
With you, I dance on banana peels,
A clumsy pair, yet oh, how it feels!

Your quirks are a jigsaw, oddly shaped,
With a corner piece gone, our plans are scraped.
We laugh at the chaos that fills the room,
In this mismatched puzzle, there's always bloom.

We're a sandwich with jelly and tuna fish,
A deliciously weird, yet absurdly swish.
Together we stumble, but it's quite alright,
For even the misfits can shine ever bright.

So sail on this ship of mismatched fate,
Through waves of calamity we celebrate.
With each silly moment, we weave our thread,
In the tapestry of two hearts, always wed.

Through the Haze of Emotion

In the fog that wraps us like a big, warm hug,
I search for wisdom, yet find only a shrug.
Your gaze, a riddle, wrapped in a grin,
Leaves me spinning, like a disco within.

With words that tumble like socks in the wash,
And misunderstandings that feel like a squash.
You say one thing, but mean something else,
Yet together we giggle at our own spells.

We toss around phrases, like confetti in fall,
And sometimes I wonder if we're both at the ball.
Your heart is a puzzle, I try to decode,
Though I often get lost on this lumpy, wild road.

With laughter our compass, we'll chase out the mist,
For every strange twist is a chance not to miss.
Together we lounge in this whimsical scene,
Through thick and through thin, we'll stay in between.

The Beat of Unsung Melodies

We hum a tune that's out of tune,
In a kitchen serenade, we dance with a spoon.
Your off-key laughter mingles with mine,
Creating harmonies that always align.

In the cluttered closet of forgotten dreams,
We find silly socks and mismatched seams.
We sing to the cat when no one is near,
While the plants shimmy, it's quite the cheer!

With rhythms that stumble, we sway to the beat,
Two clumsy musicians, oh isn't it sweet?
Every note a giggle, every rest a grin,
In this amateur concert, we revel within.

So let's keep playing, though we don't know the score,
As long as you're here, I couldn't want more.
In this waltzing uncertainty, we dance through the night,
Creating our melody with joyous delight.

Dancing Through Uncertainty

We twirl in the twilight, both dizzy and spry,
With mismatched steps underneath the sky.
Your feet tap circles while my shoes go flat,
But who cares? We laugh, keeping up with the spat!

Through puddles and petals, we skip without care,
While dodging the squirrels that scramble and glare.
In this wacky waltz, we stumble and grin,
Catching the sparkles that twinkle within.

With our heads in the clouds and our hearts in a spin,
Every misstep a chance for the giggles to win.
We glide on the surface of moments absurd,
As the song of our journey gets beautifully blurred.

So spin me around, in this whimsical ride,
With you by my side, it's a joy, a wild slide.
Amidst the uncertain, we'll find our own beat,
In a dance full of wonder, and laughter so sweet.

Shadows of Desire

In the corner, a sock lies,
Dreaming of days filled with sighs.
A flick of the tongue, a laugh lost,
What even is a relationship's cost?

Like cats in the moonlight, we dance,
Chasing whispers, missing our chance.
The pizza arrives, we rejoice,
But is it love or just the choice?

In this circus of hearts, we all bumble,
Tripping on feelings, we often stumble.
With hearts on our sleeves, so absurd,
Misunderstood dreams, how very blurred.

Yet laughter lingers as we roam,
In funny follies, we find our home.
A giggle, a wink, a shared slice,
In the mess of it all, isn't it nice?

Beneath the Veil of Uncertainty

Behind thick curtains, we play hide and seek,
What's in our hearts, we ponder and peek.
A balloon full of secrets floats above,
Is it wisdom, or just a faux love?

In the coffee shop, we share a glance,
Chickens in pajamas, missing the dance.
A scratch on the surface, a joke on the floor,
Knocking over dreams, what are we yearning for?

A yawn and a snicker, then cue the toast,
We raise our mugs, to who? Let's just boast.
With a wink and a smile, we leave it to fate,
Unraveled emotions, we giggle and wait.

Still, in the haze, there's magic to find,
With tangled connections that boggle the mind.
So let's keep it quirky, a wild mess,
Beneath the confusion, there's laughter, no less.

Kaleidoscope of Emotions

Oh, the swirl of shades in my brain,
A carousel spinning, driving me insane.
Like mixing paints, they smudge and collide,
Painting smiles and frowns, what do I hide?

The jester stands tall, with feet made of clay,
Telling me jokes in a whimsical way.
A heart-shaped piñata swings high in the air,
Break it and laugh at the silly affair.

When humor entwines with a glimmer of fate,
We're lost in a maze, oh isn't it great?
The hiccups of feelings are perfectly timed,
In this topsy-turvy, we're humorously blind.

So let's embrace this wild spectrum bright,
With giggles that twinkle like stars in the night.
For every confusion, a grin we must share,
In this whirlwind of colors, who needs to compare?

When Colors Dissonate

Notes clash and tangle, a song out of tune,
A symphony whispers beneath the big moon.
With mismatched socks and outfits gone wild,
We navigate feelings, a confused little child.

A rainbow of daffodils stuck in a dress,
Tickling the senses, a glorious mess.
Confetti of hurrahs, yet sighs in between,
Is it awkwardness, or a beautiful scene?

With puzzles of hearts, we fumble and fit,
Drawing strange patterns, never quite hit.
Through giggles and chaos, we march with a grin,
In the dissonance, together we'll spin.

So let's toast to the colors that sometimes collide,
In the mixture of moments, let's not run and hide.
For laughter's the glue that holds it all tight,
In this dazzling confusion, let's dance in the light.

Threads of the Heart

In my closet, socks collide,
A mismatched number, can't decide.
Do I wear the green or blue?
These little choices baffle too.

Dinner plans all start to shake,
Pizza's burning, oh for Pete's sake!
A salad then—oh wait, that dress!
One bite in, it's pure distress!

A text arrives, my heart does race,
But it's about my friend's pet space.
Is that a hint, or just a prank?
Guess I'll just call before I tank!

Yet through the chaos, laughter springs,
Even when stuck in tiny things.
I'll take this dance of merry fate,
And hug confusion, it's first rate!

Tides of Affection

Morning coffee, strong and bold,
Spills on shirt that's soft and old.
A heart-shaped mug does misbehave,
As if to say, 'You're just a knave!'

Dinner dates arranged with flair,
But oops! I brought a cat to share.
The waiter laughed, said, 'What a sight!'
Next time, I'll keep it out of sight.

Unexpected smiles on crowded trains,
But do they see my crazy veins?
Giggling at the stranger's tie,
Should I wave or just say goodbye?

Yet waves of joy come crashing down,
When strangers share a smile, no frown.
In midst of jokes and simple cheer,
I'll ride these tides with no clear steer!

The Poetry of Conflicted Wishes

I want to sleep, but snacks allure,
A midnight feast would be the cure.
Yet in this battle, chips do scream,
Against my pillow—what a dream!

A song that plays upon repeat,
But should I dance or claim my seat?
Bump into friends, a sudden pause,
'Can I join you?' a hopeful cause.

Lost in texts, the screen does glow,
Are they my friends or just a show?
With auto-correct spelling woes,
It's like I'm trapped in silly prose!

But oh, the laughter that ensues,
Makes tangled thoughts something to amuse.
With whims that swirl and thoughts that mesh,
I'll twirl and spin, no need to fresh!

Unraveled Threads

Knitting purls that turn to knots,
My blanket looks like crumbled thoughts.
Each row a tale of tangled yarn,
With patterns lost, oh how I yawn!

Emails sent but never read,
A mystery where penguins tread.
"Did I really hit send?" I muse,
While laughing at my absent clues.

Plans to meet drawn on a map,
Somehow I wound up in a nap.
Calling friends to share my fate,
"The pizza's late, but that's just great!"

In this jumbled weave of glee,
I'll take the stitches folded free.
For every twist is just a laugh,
In this grand chaos, I find my path!

Singularity of the Heart

In a world of chocolate sprinkles,
We dance on jellybeans, what a sprinkle!
With socks that never match each day,
We giggle as we lose our way.

Cupcakes line the streets, so sweet,
We trip on icing with our feet.
Oh, such a twist, a tumble here,
But joy ignites, it's crystal clear.

In this carnival of zany sights,
We ride the merry-go-round of nights.
With every spin, our heads do whirl,
Oh darling, take my hand, let's twirl!

Through ups and downs, we board the train,
Where laughter spills and wipes the pain.
With silly hats and gummy bears,
We find our bliss, forget our cares.

Echoes of Heartstrings

In kitchen chaos, pots do clash,
Yet somehow comes a tasty mash.
With every chop, a laugh erupts,
We're cooking love, all mixed up!

As socks parade in a footwear show,
The mismatched styles steal the glow.
With each silly glance, a giggle springs,
In this concert of odd little things.

With sticky notes as our love notes,
We sail on bubbles, ride on boats.
In a sea of popcorn, we float and drift,
Embracing chaos, our favorite gift.

Painting dreams with colors bold,
Our oddball tales never get old.
Though the world spins, we hold tight,
In this dance, everything feels right.

Whispers in a Chaotic Mind

In a circus of thoughts, we often juggle,
Clowns and acrobats, oh what a muddle!
With a wink, a nudge, we laugh so loud,
As ideas flock, like a wild crowd.

With mismatched socks and peanut snacks,
We ride the rollercoaster, no time to relax.
Through twists and turns, we find delight,
In the mess of things, we take flight.

Voices clash like jazz gone wrong,
Yet somehow it still feels like a song.
Oh, how the rhythm keeps us spinning,
In this quirky game, we're always winning!

With thoughts that dance, like shadows cast,
In this madcap world, we're unsurpassed.
Through laughs and sighs, we journey far,
With silliness lighting every bizarre.

The Tangle of Moments

In a web of giggles, we're caught up tight,
Pulling on string with all our might.
We trip on memories, can't find our shoes,
In this funny maze, we just can't lose.

With rubber ducks and flying kites,
We race through puddles, oh what sights!
Each blink a chance to laugh anew,
In a whirl of madness, just me and you.

Through juggling pies and silly hats,
Our minds spin wild, amidst the spats.
Yet every twist brings joy so bright,
In this tangle, everything feels right.

In this carnival, we'll cling and play,
With every moment, we'll find our way.
Through ups and downs, we'll laugh till dawn,
In this crazy dance, we'll carry on.

The Dance of Heartbeats

In a room with too much chatter,
Two hearts thump in a scattered patter.
They trip on feet, laugh, then collide,
Who knew a dance could slip and slide?

A bowl of fruit, some mismatched pairs,
Avoided by the cat who stares.
Lemon peels and giggles loud,
An accidental waltz, awkwardly proud.

The clock ticks on, they lose all sense,
Time's a joke, and it's intense.
With every beat, the rhythm sways,
In this chaotic, merry maze.

As laughter fades, they share a glance,
Is it a friendship or silly romance?
Tripping through this funny game,
With heartbeats dancing, never the same.

Fractured Dreams

A jigsaw dream in disarray,
Pieces placed the wrong way.
I wish for sunshine, get the rain,
Windows open, yet it's all insane.

My pasta sings with too much sauce,
A carton of milk? I am the boss.
Mixing flavors, a recipe strange,
It's a meal, or a game, it's hard to gauge.

In my head, thoughts bounce like balls,
A clown's parade in mismatched halls.
Confetti dreams in a paper kite,
Flying high and taking flight.

Who knows when the puzzle's back?
Until then, I'll ride this whack.
Fractured visions waltz in sync,
With every sip, I stop and think.

The Labyrinth of Yearning

In a maze with twists and turns,
Searching for what my heart yearns.
Every corner hides a face,
Each step brings a new embrace.

The map is drawn in crayon bright,
Spots of laughter light the night.
A duck on roller skates passes by,
Is it an illusion, or did I fly?

Chasing shadows, it's a game,
Crisps of autumn call my name.
Where's the exit? Who can say?
I'm lost in giggles, come what may.

A riddle whispered, a song to dance,
Each misstep gives a second chance.
Through winding paths, together we roam,
In this quirky maze, we've found our home.

Serendipity's Enigma

A chance encounter, oh what a scene,
Tripped over a cat, if you know what I mean.
With cookies flying, and laughter wide,
In this puzzle of fate, we slide and glide.

A banana peel? A sudden fall?
Turns an awkward moment into a ball.
Socks mismatched, a fashion faux pas,
Yet here's a grin, without a flaw.

Coffee spills on a map unrolled,
Settings for stories yet untold.
In the chaos, a spark ignites,
Two silly hearts on wondrous nights.

With every blunder, the threads entwine,
A tapestry stitched from the divine.
In the waltz of quirks, we find our place,
In this grand enigma, we share a space.

Silent Liaisons

In a crowded room we dance so near,
Yet whispers fade while laughs disappear.
We exchange glances, the jokes unsaid,
A sock puppet nods, wishing we wed.

You say my name as the cat trips by,
I toss a wink, you pretend to cry.
With every giggle, the truth feels shy,
Like my old fridge, it's warm, oh my!

We play charades with our hearts on fire,
Yet always miss the flaming desire.
A mime throws roses, what a weird game,
But darling, it's fun, let's blame the fame.

So here we stand, awkward but bold,
In our silent ballet, a story unfolds.
With every chuckle, the night wears thin,
Who knew confusion could feel like a win?

A Journey Through Tangled Paths

In the woods, a sign points right or left,
But every choice feels like a jest.
We stroll on paths where the squirrels mock,
And laugh at us while they gather their stock.

With maps all crumpled and compasses broke,
We end up lost in a cloud of smoke.
A rabbit points out the way to roam,
Claiming it leads back to our cozy home.

Yet every corner brings more surprise,
Where balloons float high in the silly skies.
Chasing dreams made of bubblegum,
With giggles galore, here we come!

So here's to the trips that never end,
With each new twist, we find a friend.
Through tangled woods, we run with glee,
In this chaotic dance, just you and me!

Reflections in a Glassy Pond

Beside the pond where lilies prance,
We throw in coins as we joke and dance.
With every splash, our wishes collide,
Creating ripples where secrets hide.

Your eyes like marbles, bright and round,
In their depths, my thoughts are drowned.
A frog leaps by, croaking witty lines,
As we ponder life's odd designs.

Each ripple tells tales we cannot share,
Of hiccuped moments and snorted air.
We laugh till dawn at the fish's plight,
Who gave up hope of taking flight.

So let's keep tossing our dreams for fun,
Into this pond where stories run.
For in the reflections that shimmer and bend,
Lies the humor we find with our hearts to mend.

Uncharted Maps of Emotion

With crayons in hand, we draw our hearts,
But the ink spills over, confusing the parts.
Each map we sketch leads us in circles,
Winding through valleys of mischievous giggles.

An X marks the spot, or so we supposed,
But the treasure found was just an old hose.
We wrap it around for a game of frisbee,
While laughing so hard, my pants got breezy.

Through maze-like feelings, we run up and down,
In this carnival of odd, we're the clowns.
A slip on a banana, a trip on a slide,
In these uncharted lands, our joy won't hide.

So here's to the paths we craft with delight,
In this wacky adventure, everything feels right.
For in the chaos and curves that we roam,
We find silly maps that lead us back home.

The Echoes of Tomorrow

When socks go missing, it's quite a scene,
The dryer whispers secrets, oh what could it mean?
With empty mugs marking a coffee spree,
Mysteries dance like shadows, wild and free.

Time slips like a fish, it's hard to hold tight,
One minute a sneeze, next it's midnight!
Our plans do a tango, twirling about,
As we chase dreams dressed in pajamas, no doubt.

The cat has opinions, as cats often do,
On mysteries of snacks and which toy is new.
While the plants in the corner start plotting their spree,
To grow up and mock us, with glee and esprit.

So let's raise a toast to the baffling quest,
With laughter our shield, we're surely the best!
In the chaos of now, where questions do bloom,
We laugh at the echoes that burst in the room.

Tethered to the Unknown

With mismatched shoes and a cup for a hat,
I wade through confusion, just look at that!
The directions are jumbled, a puzzle to solve,
While whispers of reason begin to dissolve.

A calendar's got flair, with colors galore,
Yet details elude me, leave me wanting more.
As moments collide, like a pie in the face,
I tiptoe through echoes of a baffling race.

So here's to the journeys that lead us astray,
With laughter our guide, we'll find our own way.
Through maps of dot-dash that no one could read,
We'll dance to the rhythm of joy's silly seed.

In the tangle of paths that we wander each day,
We'll chuckle and smile, come what may.
For tangled confusion's a canvas anew,
With colors of laughter, just waiting for you!

The Canvas of Unfinished Stories

With crayons and scribbles, our tales take flight,
An empty canvas awaits, eager for light.
The brush strokes of giggles blend hues of delight,
As we weave through the chaos, ready for night.

The plot twists are wild, like spaghetti on cliffs,
Characters pop up with some comical rifts.
Why's the frog in a tux? What a curious choice!
In this world of whimsy, we give dreams a voice.

So grab your odd socks and dance on the edge,
With laughter our compass, we're bound to hedge.
An unfinished tale, yet perfectly grand,
We scribble and giggle, hand in hand.

And when the page flips, as it surely will do,
We'll toast to the stories that never feel due.
A canvas of heartstrings, with shades of the absurd,
Together we'll laugh, in our odd little world.

Reverie of Unspoken Words

In a world without whispers, we chuckle and grin,
With thoughts a wild river, where do we begin?
Our minds throw a party, confetti galore,
Yet meaning gets lost, oh what a chore!

With smiles like beacons, we're lost in the fray,
Our minds do a shuffle, come what may.
The silent exchanges, so quirky and bright,
Turn laughter to echoes that dance through the night.

The pause and the stammer, like bubbles in tea,
Make wit rise to levels that stab at the glee.
In the space where we fumble, so playful and warm,
We find joy in the chaos, a beautiful storm.

So here's to the moments that balance on tongue,
With laughter as our anthem, forever we're young.
In the reverie of thoughts that tumble and twirl,
We'll cherish the comedy in this baffling swirl.

Beneath the Surface of Desire

In a sea of hearts, I swim and dive,
Sorting through feelings, trying to thrive.
With wishful dreams in a fish bowl jar,
I chase the sweet scent of a candy bar.

Bubbles of giggles float like balloons,
While I trip on words like clumsy tunes.
Tangled in thoughts like spaghetti strands,
I seek out the sun with unsteady hands.

A crush on a smile, a wink in the air,
All jumbled emotions mix everywhere.
The pie chart of heartbeats spins a wild show,
Hopeful on Mondays, confused by the flow.

But in this circus, I find my grace,
With joy in the chaos, I'm learning to pace.
Even spaghetti can twirl and delight,
As I laugh through the mess, dancing in light.

Flickers of a Jumbled Mind

Lights flicker fast like a mind on a spree,
Puzzle pieces scattered, where could they be?
A thought about lunch, then a cat with a hat,
Each jump of my brain's like a wild acrobat.

Coffee cups swirling, ideas to chase,
A whirlwind of nonsense, like a dizzy race.
Playful delusions dance in my head,
As I try to remember my dreams from the bed.

A calendar full, yet much still to do,
My focus is shifting, like the colors of blue.
In the middle of chaos, a giggle erupts,
How funny life spins when it suddenly disrupts.

Yet laughter comes easy through all of the fuss,
Navigating the wild that's continual plus.
In the jumbled confusion, a sparkle I find,
A flicker of joy in this whimsical mind.

When Stars Align in Chaos

Stars scatter widely, like socks in a dryer,
One minute you're soaring, the next a high flyer.
Synchronizing mishaps, a dance in the night,
With partners like flops, oh what a sight!

Fate flips a coin, and it lands on its edge,
Juggling intentions while standing on a ledge.
With laughter the glue, and quirks as the spice,
Navigating mayhem can be rather nice.

The cosmos conspire with pizza in hand,
While I count the jellybeans stuck in the sand.
Wishes once whispered now shout from the rooftops,
In the tangle of stardust, the laughter never stops.

So here's to the chaos, the mess we embrace,
When stars take a break, we still find our place.
For even in madness, we find a grand cheer,
Twisting through trouble, we hold each other near.

The Currency of Emotions

Trading small glances as if they were gold,
A smile for a hug, stories untold.
In this barter of hearts, I lend you my glee,
While you hand me a laugh just for being free.

A currency flows as I slip on my shoes,
From coffee shop musings to silly views.
Counted in giggles, with joy on the side,
Each moment I treasure, my heart's open wide.

The winks of a stranger, a wave from a friend,
Each deal brings a sparkle, a message to send.
In the market of feelings, I'm rich as can be,
With pockets of laughter and a heart full of glee.

So let's trade our stories, our quirks and delight,
In the bazaar of whimsy, everything feels right.
For in this together, we share and we grow,
The currency of feelings, the best way to flow.

Eclipsed by Enchantment

In the midst of clowns and jest,
A jingle played, a curious quest.
Chasing shadows, tripping toes,
The night revealed what no one knows.

The moon wore shoes, a hat so bright,
Dancing freely, what a sight!
Jumbled thoughts, a dizzy spin,
A laugh erupts, where to begin?

We twirled beneath a painted sky,
As giggles soared and dreams flew high.
Wobbly truths, a chuckle wide,
Lost in the whims we dared to ride.

Yet in this chaos, hearts did sing,
With every pratfall, joy they'd bring.
Missteps left us all bemused,
In delightful mess, we felt so used.

Bridging the Unseen

A bridge was built with silly threads,
As thoughts danced 'round like tiny reds.
Wobbling paths, we crossed with glee,
What's on the other side? Let's see!

Through tangled vines and whispers loud,
A friendly squawk, a curious crowd.
Puzzles bent, and ideas tossed,
In the ruckus, we counted the cost.

Flying high on paper planes,
Through dotted lines and mental trains.
The view was worth the funny fall,
As we rumbled on, we'd sway through it all.

Twists and turns, like candy cane,
In this circus, joy was our gain.
With smiles wide, we leaped and skipped,
On the unseen paths, we all equipped.

Constellations in Disguise

Stars wore hats and danced in pairs,
Glances met with curious stares.
A comet tripped, fell on the moon,
What a sight, a crazy tune!

Navigating with a quirky chart,
Each twinkle tugging at the heart.
Mysteries wrapped in glitter threads,
Led us on as laughter spreads.

Through the milky ways of odd delight,
We hired ghosts to guide our flight.
Mirthful echoes in the night sky,
With sparkling grins, we dared to fly.

Yet in the dark, the paths entwined,
With every laugh, a truth defined.
In cosmic jest, we all must play,
As constellations light the way.

Echoes of Uncertainty

In a hall of echoes, we all laugh,
Chasing shadows, doing the math.
What's next? We just can't decide,
As quicksand thoughts began to slide.

Questions bounced off the wobbly walls,
Each answer hid, threw silent calls.
Cracking up at the mystery's fire,
We spun around in our chaos choir.

Mirrors reflecting our puzzled faces,
In the garden of odd embraces.
Fumbling through the sticky maze,
As laughter filled the puzzled haze.

With every twist, a chuckle penned,
In the confetti of thought, we'd blend.
Though veiled in mystery, we all say,
This wild ride is the only way.

Threads of Fate

In the dance of socks that mysteriously stray,
One's always lost, while the other finds a way.
Like mismatched shoes that waltz with a grin,
Stumbling through the chaos, where do we begin?

Balloons chase after a gusty little breeze,
Tickling our noses, as we laugh with ease.
Spinning in circles, we bump into walls,
Yet somehow keep giggling at our foolish falls.

A Symphony of Questions

Why do ducks march in a line so neat?
Are they heading somewhere, or just feeling the beat?
With each quack they sound like they know the score,
While we wonder aloud, "What's this all for?"

As clouds drift and ponder what shape they should take,
Do they have a plan, or just wing it for fun's sake?
The sun looks confused, playing peek-a-boo,
While we sip our coffee, puzzling life's brew.

The Puzzle of Affection

With pieces that jigsaw our hearts into place,
Sometimes they fit well, sometimes they leave a trace.
Like cats that ignore us, yet claim all the space,
While we chase little whispers that finally embrace.

A smile at the wrong time can cause a short laugh,
Like a math problem solved by a silly giraffe.
We fumble through moments, both sticky and bright,
Yet find that the laughter is worth every fight.

Mirages of the Soul

In the desert of thoughts where the cacti grow tall,
Mirages of whims come to tease and to call.
With shadows that flicker and dance in the sand,
We chase after rainbows, but they slip from our hand.

A mirage of meetings, where hugs turn to pranks,
As we trip over dreams, and laugh with our flanks.
Yet in the wild twist of our untamed parade,
We find gems of joy in the mess that we made.

Stardust of Mistaken Paths

In the garden of socks, I lost my shoe,
Pondering if missteps were part of the view.
Cats hold meetings, they conspire with glee,
As I trip over thoughts, oh dear, not the tea!

Maps made of jelly, they wiggle and sway,
Guiding me onward in a quirky ballet.
I chase after whispers that promise delight,
But all I can find is a mist in the night.

The moon's got a secret; I bet it's a joke,
While I juggle my dreams with a balancing poke.
Frogs play the banjo, they serenade flies,
And the stars laugh in twinkles, oh, what a surprise!

Yet somehow these blunders create such a show,
A jester's parade where the oddities flow.
With each clumsy step, I'm discovering truth,
That silliness dances with wisdom uncouth.

Embracing the Unknown

Waking up wondering which shoe to wear,
The left one's a rebel; the right one's quite fair.
Coffee spills laughter on my morning attire,
As I search for my keys, which I can't seem to acquire.

The toaster's a psychic; it knows how I feel,
Burnt toast or a masterpiece, tell me, what's real?
Socks in strange pairings, they wave from the drawer,
As I dance with my breakfast, seeking out more.

Thought bubbles drift like balloons in the sky,
Pop one and giggle; oh my, oh my!
I trip over wisdom hidden in fluff,
And embrace the confusion with just a bit of gruff.

So here's to adventures not mapped out in ink,
Let's swirl through the chaos and not even think.
Between hugs of the silly, there's clarity too,
In the muddle of moments, I discover what's true.

Chasing Fireflies in Twilight

Beneath the glow of stars, I'm running in glee,
Chasing bright flashes like dots on a spree.
In the evening's embrace, confusion takes flight,
While giggles and whispers ignite the delight.

Lightning bugs twinkle, they dance with a wink,
As I trip over shadows, my thoughts start to sink.
These tiny illuminations all flicker and tease,
They lead me in circles, oh what a breeze!

I've lost track of time; is it late or too soon?
When crickets decide it's their time for a tune.
There's magic in missteps, a spark that ignites,
In the funk of the confusion, I twirl with the nights.

So gather your laughter, let's all join the chase,
In the game of the silly, there's never a race.
With fireflies guiding us, we laugh till we drop,
In this whimsical journey, we'll never stop!

The Puzzle of Affection

Two peas in a pod found a runaway shoe,
While mismatched odd socks made their debut.
A riddle of giggles wrapped tight like a hug,
As hearts play charades, giving out a warm shrug.

Each clue is a wink, sweet secrets unfold,
Like bananas in pajamas, they're playful and bold.
Tickle me silly as we spin in a whirl,
With every surprise twist, watch the chaos unfurl!

The brain's like a jigsaw, pieces astray,
Comical fragments that brighten the day.
Playing with puzzles that never quite fit,
But kindness and chuckles make each piece a hit!

So let's toast to the oddballs that shape this big game,
Fizzing like soda, it's never the same.
In the tangles of riddles, we're guided by cheer,
Finding warmth in the moments we hold most dear.

The Ripple of Hope

In a world full of oddities,
We chase after giggles and glee,
With each twist and turn we make,
Laughter's the shortcut, you see.

A tumble, a fumble, we slip and slide,
Chasing our dreams like they're lost at sea,
Yet each splash and a splashback we ride,
Carving a masterpiece of comedy.

Balloons float past with the grace of a dance,
Bumping our heads, we feign a romance,
Despite all the mess, we take a stance,
Every blunder a laugh, a chance to enhance.

So here's to the ones who trip and fall,
Finding joy in the chaos, after all,
For as we navigate this wacky hall,
We discover the treasures in every close call.

Navigating Through Whispers

In the hush of the night, secrets are shared,
Rumors take flight like a cat that's unpaired,
We giggle at tales that barely make sense,
As we tiptoe through echoes, on laughter's defense.

With whispers of nonsense floating around,
We search for the truth, but it never is found,
Every chuckle disguises a twist in our fate,
Dancing with shadows, it's never too late.

A misstep in thought makes the crowd roar with glee,
For what is a joke if it's not a wee spree?
Navigating the currents of playful debate,
Each word like a ripple, it's never too late.

So toast to the chaos that keeps us awake,
To whispers and giggles that never mistake,
For in every small pause, a story will break,
And we'll laugh through the night for our own silly sake.

Swaying in Turbulent Winds

In the gusts of the day, we sway to a tune,
Like piñatas afloat under the light of the moon,
Wobbling 'round corners, we spin and we roll,
Catching the breeze with our heart and our soul.

Crowds gather 'round to see what we'll do,
We erupt into smiles as confusion ensues,
With every wild turn and a skip in our step,
We feast on the folly, our own little rep.

Chaotic and merry, we triumphantly yell,
With every odd moment, we conjure a spell,
For life is a circus with ups and with downs,
And we're just the jesters in baffling gowns.

So let's waltz through the chaos, twirl on a whim,
There's joy in the mess, let the laughter begin,
As long as we're swaying, we're never alone,
In the turbulent winds, we have found our home.

The Harmony of Disarray

Amidst the clatter, bells ring and chime,
We dance in the madness, it's hilariously prime,
Finding rhythm in chaos, a song out of tune,
Twisting and leaping, we're just past noon.

With mismatched socks and a grin that won't quit,
We tumble through moments that don't quite fit,
Every wrong note plays, a symphonic delight,
In the echoes of laughter, we soar to new heights.

Containers of sizzle serve meals far from bland,
As we juggle our juggling with a clumsy hand,
The orchestra plays, our spirits take flight,
In the harmony made when the world isn't right.

So here's to the jumbles that keep us in tune,
To finding our joy in the midst of the swoon,
For every discord blossoms a sweet bouquet,
In the grand show of life, we choose to parlay.

Heartbeats in the Chaos

In a world that spins like a top,
We dance through the mess, can't stop.
With socks mismatched and hair a fright,
We stumble on through day and night.

Cereal spills on the kitchen floor,
We laugh as we clean, then we roar.
Bills piled high like a tower of glee,
Yet somehow, we just feel so free.

A cat on the counter, a dog in the sink,
We ponder our choices while we drink.
With laughter echoing through every room,
Adventures bloom amid the gloom.

So here's to the quirks that make us whole,
Those baffling moments that spark the soul.
In the crazy swirl, we find our pace,
Two hearts racing in a jumbled space.

A Whisper in the Wind

As autumn leaves pirouette and sway,
Whispers twist in the breeze at play.
A squirrel debates which nut to claim,
While we ponder much deeper things, just the same.

Cup of coffee or a slice of pie,
With every choice, we sigh and cry.
Should we dance in the rain or stay dry?
Oh, the absurdity that makes us high.

A wink from the stranger on the street,
The questions that fizzle from every greet.
Is it charm or a trick of the mind?
We tumble on, blissfully blind.

In the middle of chaos, we find a tune,
Laughing together beneath the moon.
Echoing giggles, our hearts entwined,
In whispers and chuckles, confusion is kind.

Bridges Built on Dreams

Constructing bridges made of fluff,
With hopes held high, never enough.
We leap and bounce, defy the fall,
While kittens plot how to conquer all.

With crayons spilled on the office floor,
We scribble futures we can't ignore.
The landmarks shift as we giggle along,
Creating paths where we all belong.

In the sandbox of wishes, towers rise,
As ice cream melts under sun-splashed skies.
A hiccup here, a giggle there,
Navigating this maze, with hardly a care.

So let's build castles with nonsense bricks,
Where tomfoolery and dreams do mix.
Facing the wild with hearts so bold,
Spin round and round, let the stories unfold.

The Weight of Unspoken Words

In silence thick as peanut butter,
We juggle secrets, hearts in a flutter.
Eyeing that slice of cake so high,
Words stuck fast, we just sigh.

Crammed with thoughts like a suitcase full,
We tiptoe around the golden rule.
A wink here, a laugh there too,
Navigating riddles that sometimes ensue.

The burden of phrases we never shared,
Like morning coffee, slightly impaired.
Yet between the bites, we find a way,
To express the sweet in our own array.

With impromptu dances in grocery aisles,
And everyday mishaps that spark our smiles,
The tales we craft in this silly whirl,
Paint the world bright in a tangled twirl.

www.ingramcontent.com/pod-product-compliance
Lightning Source LLC
Chambersburg PA
CBHW051631160426
43209CB00004B/601